Table of Contents

Brunch for a Bunch

*Go and enjoy choice food and sweet drinks,
and send some to those who have nothing
prepared....The joy of the Lord is your strength.*
Nehemiah 8:10 NIV

Aunt Marilyn's Cinnamon French Toast Casserole

1 large loaf French bread, cut into 1½-inch slices
3½ cups milk
9 eggs
1½ cups sugar, divided
1 tablespoon vanilla
½ teaspoon salt
6 to 8 medium baking apples, such as McIntosh or
    Cortland, peeled and sliced
1 teaspoon ground cinnamon
½ teaspoon ground nutmeg
    Powdered sugar (optional)

1. Place bread slices in greased 13×9-inch glass baking dish or casserole.

2. Whisk milk, eggs, 1 cup sugar, vanilla and salt in large bowl until well blended. Pour half of mixture over bread. Layer apple slices over bread. Pour remaining half of egg mixture over apples.

3. Combine remaining ½ cup sugar, cinnamon and nutmeg in small bowl; sprinkle over casserole. Cover and refrigerate overnight.

4. Preheat oven to 350°F. Bake 1 hour or until egg mixture is set. Sprinkle with powdered sugar.

Makes 6 to 8 servings

Breakfast Bake

   1 pound ground pork sausage
   1 teaspoon Italian seasoning
   ½ teaspoon salt
   6 eggs
   2 cups milk
   ½ cup CREAM OF WHEAT® Hot Cereal (Instant, 1-minute, 2½-minute
       or 10-minute cook time), uncooked
   1 teaspoon TRAPPEY'S® Red Devil™ Cayenne Pepper Sauce
   4 cups cubed bread stuffing (potato bread recommended)
   2 cups Cheddar cheese, shredded

1. Brown sausage in skillet, pressing with fork or spatula to crumble as it cooks. Sprinkle on Italian seasoning and salt; set aside.

2. Combine eggs, milk, Cream of Wheat and pepper sauce in large mixing bowl; mix well. Add cooked sausage and bread stuffing; toss to combine. Pour mixture into 13×9-inch casserole pan; cover. Refrigerate at least 4 hours or overnight.

3. Preheat oven to 350°F. Remove cover and sprinkle cheese over casserole. Cover pan with aluminum foil; bake 30 minutes. Remove foil; bake 15 minutes longer. Serve warm.   *Makes 8 servings*

Serving Suggestion: Serve this dish with fresh fruit.

Prep Time: 30 minutes
Start to Finish Time: 4 to 12 hours soaking, 45 minutes baking

Ham 'n' Apple Breakfast Casserole Slices

   1 package (15 ounces) refrigerated pie crusts (2 crusts)
  20 pieces (about 1 pound) thinly sliced ham, cut into bite-size pieces
   1 can (21 ounces) apple pie filling
   1 cup (4 ounces) shredded sharp Cheddar cheese
   ¼ cup plus 1 teaspoon sugar, divided
   ½ teaspoon ground cinnamon

1. Preheat oven to 425°F.

2. Place one crust in 9-inch pie pan, allowing edges to hang over sides. Arrange half of ham pieces in bottom. Spoon apple pie filling over ham. Arrange remaining ham on top of apples; cover with cheese.

continued on page 6

Ham 'n' Apple Breakfast Casserole Slices, continued

3. Mix ¼ cup sugar and cinnamon in small bowl; sprinkle evenly over cheese. Arrange second crust over filling and crimp edges together. Brush crust lightly with water and sprinkle with remaining 1 teaspoon sugar. Cut slits in top for steam to escape.

4. Bake 20 to 25 minutes or until crust is golden brown. Cool 15 minutes. Slice into wedges.
Makes 6 servings

Note: This casserole can be assembled the night before, covered and refrigerated, then baked the next morning.

Pineapple Coffee Cake

    1 can (20 ounces) DOLE® Pineapple Chunks
    ½ cup packed brown sugar
    1 teaspoon ground cinnamon
    ½ cup chopped walnuts
    3 tablespoons butter or margarine, diced
    2 cups prepared baking mix
    2 tablespoons granulated sugar
    1 egg

• Drain pineapple, reserve ⅔ cup juice. Pat pineapple dry.

• Mix brown sugar, cinnamon, walnuts and butter in medium bowl; set aside.

• Beat reserved juice with baking mix, granulated sugar and egg in large bowl for 30 seconds. Spoon into 9-inch round baking pan sprayed with nonstick vegetable cooking spray. Top with half of walnut mixture, pineapple and remaining walnut mixture.

• Bake at 400°F. 20 to 25 minutes. Cool.
Makes 8 servings

Prep Time: 20 minutes
Bake Time: 25 minutes

Brunch Eggs Olé

8 eggs
½ cup all-purpose flour
1 teaspoon baking powder
¾ teaspoon salt
2 cups (8 ounces) shredded Monterey Jack cheese with jalapeño peppers
1½ cups (12 ounces) small curd cottage cheese
1 cup (4 ounces) shredded sharp Cheddar cheese
1 jalapeño pepper,* seeded and chopped
½ teaspoon hot pepper sauce
Fresh Salsa (recipe follows)

*Jalapeño peppers can sting and irritate the skin, so wear rubber gloves when handling peppers and do not touch your eyes.

1. Preheat oven to 350°F. Grease 9-inch square baking pan.

2. Beat eggs in large bowl with electric mixer at high speed 4 to 5 minutes or until slightly thickened and lemon-colored. Combine flour, baking powder and salt in small bowl. Stir flour mixture into eggs until blended.

3. Combine Monterey Jack cheese, cottage cheese, Cheddar cheese, jalapeño and hot pepper sauce in medium bowl; mix well. Fold into egg mixture until well blended. Pour into prepared pan.

4. Bake 45 to 50 minutes or until golden brown and firm in center. Meanwhile, prepare Fresh Salsa. Let stand 10 minutes before cutting into squares. Serve with salsa.

Makes 8 servings

Fresh Salsa

3 medium plum tomatoes, seeded and chopped
2 tablespoons chopped onion
1 small jalapeño pepper,* stemmed, seeded and minced
1 tablespoon chopped fresh cilantro
1 tablespoon lime juice
¼ teaspoon salt
⅛ teaspoon black pepper

*Jalapeño peppers can sting and irritate the skin, so wear rubber gloves when handling peppers and do not touch your eyes.

Combine tomatoes, onion, jalapeño, cilantro, lime juice, salt and black pepper in small bowl. Cover and refrigerate until ready to serve.

Makes 1 cup

Cranberry Coffee Cake

½ **cup walnuts or pecans, coarsely chopped, toasted***
¾ **cup sugar, divided**
1 **cup plus 1 tablespoon all-purpose flour, divided**
½ **cup (1 stick) plus 1 tablespoon butter, softened, divided**
½ **teaspoon ground cinnamon**
½ **teaspoon baking soda**
½ **teaspoon baking powder**
½ **teaspoon salt**
1 **egg**
2 **to 3 teaspoons grated orange peel**
½ **teaspoon vanilla**
½ **cup sour cream**
⅔ **cup dried cranberries**

To toast nuts, spread in single layer on ungreased baking sheet. Bake in preheated 350°F oven 5 to 7 minutes or until lightly browned, stirring once.

1. Preheat oven to 350°F. Grease and flour 8-inch square baking dish.

2. For topping, combine walnuts, ¼ cup sugar, 1 tablespoon flour, 1 tablespoon butter and cinnamon in small bowl; rub mixture with fingertips until well blended.

3. Sift remaining 1 cup flour, baking soda, baking powder and salt into medium bowl. Beat remaining ½ cup sugar and ½ cup butter in large bowl with electric mixer at medium-high speed 2 to 3 minutes or until light and fluffy. Add egg, orange peel and vanilla; mix well.

4. Alternately add flour mixture and sour cream to sugar mixture; beat at low speed until blended. *Do not overmix.* Fold in cranberries. Spread batter in prepared pan; sprinkle with topping.

5. Bake 25 to 30 minutes or until toothpick inserted into center comes out clean. Cool 5 minutes before cutting.   *Makes 16 servings*

Chocolate Chunk Coffee Cake

1¾ cups all-purpose flour
1 teaspoon baking powder
1 teaspoon baking soda
½ teaspoon salt
¾ cup packed brown sugar
½ cup (1 stick) butter, softened
3 eggs
1 teaspoon vanilla
1 cup sour cream
1 package (about 11 ounces) semisweet chocolate chunks
1 cup chopped nuts

1. Preheat oven to 350°F. Grease 13×9-inch baking pan.

2. Combine flour, baking powder, baking soda and salt in medium bowl. Beat brown sugar and butter in large bowl with electric mixer at medium speed until creamy. Add eggs and vanilla; beat until well blended. Alternately add flour mixture and sour cream; beat until blended. Stir in chocolate chunks and nuts. Spread batter evenly in prepared pan.

3. Bake 25 to 35 minutes or until toothpick inserted into center comes out clean. Cool in pan on wire rack.   *Makes about 18 servings*

Summer Sausage 'n' Egg Wedges

4 eggs, beaten
⅓ cup milk
¼ cup all-purpose flour
½ teaspoon baking powder
⅛ teaspoon garlic powder
2½ cups (10 ounces) shredded Cheddar or mozzarella cheese, divided
1½ cups diced HILLSHIRE FARM® Summer Sausage
1 cup cream-style cottage cheese with chives

Preheat oven to 375°F.

Combine eggs, milk, flour, baking powder and garlic powder in medium bowl; beat until combined. Stir in 2 cups Cheddar cheese, Summer Sausage and cottage cheese. Pour into greased 9-inch pie plate. Bake, uncovered, 25 to 30 minutes or until golden and knife inserted into center comes out clean. To serve, cut into 6 wedges. Sprinkle wedges with remaining ½ cup Cheddar cheese.   *Makes 6 servings*

Chocolate Chunk Coffee Cake

Spinach Sensation

½ pound bacon slices
1 cup (8 ounces) sour cream
3 eggs, separated
2 tablespoons all-purpose flour
⅛ teaspoon black pepper
1 package (10 ounces) frozen chopped spinach,
    thawed and squeezed dry
½ cup (2 ounces) shredded sharp Cheddar cheese
½ cup dry bread crumbs
1 tablespoon butter, melted

1. Preheat oven to 350°F. Spray 9-inch round baking dish with nonstick cooking spray.

2. Place bacon in single layer in large skillet; cook over medium heat until crisp. Remove from skillet; drain on paper towels. Crumble and set aside.

3. Combine sour cream, egg yolks, flour and pepper in large bowl; set aside. Beat egg whites in medium bowl with electric mixer at high speed until stiff peaks form. Stir one fourth of egg whites into sour cream mixture; fold in remaining egg whites.

4. Arrange half of spinach in prepared dish. Top with half of sour cream mixture. Sprinkle ¼ cup cheese over sour cream mixture. Sprinkle bacon over cheese. Repeat layers, ending with remaining ¼ cup cheese.

5. Combine bread crumbs and butter in small bowl; sprinkle evenly over cheese. Bake 30 to 35 minutes or until egg mixture is set. Let stand 5 minutes before serving. Garnish as desired.

Makes 6 servings

Nutty Toffee Coffee Cake

1⅓ cups (8-ounce package) HEATH® BITS 'O BRICKLE™ Toffee Bits, divided
⅓ cup plus ¾ cup packed light brown sugar, divided
2¼ cups all-purpose flour, divided
9 tablespoons butter or margarine, softened and divided
¾ cup granulated sugar
2 teaspoons baking powder
½ teaspoon ground cinnamon
¼ teaspoon salt
1¼ cups milk
1 egg
1 teaspoon vanilla extract
¾ cup chopped nuts

1. Heat oven to 350°F. Grease and flour 13×9×2-inch baking pan. Stir together ½ cup toffee bits, ⅓ cup brown sugar, ¼ cup flour and 3 tablespoons butter. Stir until crumbly; set aside.

2. Combine remaining 2 cups flour, granulated sugar, remaining ¾ cup brown sugar, remaining 6 tablespoons butter, baking powder, cinnamon and salt in large mixer bowl; mix until well blended. Gradually add milk, egg and vanilla, beating until thoroughly blended. Stir in remaining toffee bits and nuts. Spread batter in prepared pan.

3. Sprinkle reserved crumb topping over batter. Bake 30 to 35 minutes or until wooden pick inserted in center comes out clean. Serve warm or cool.

Makes 12 to 16 servings

Bacon and Maple Grits Puff

8 slices bacon
2 cups milk
1¼ cups water
1 cup uncooked quick-cooking grits
½ teaspoon salt
½ cup maple syrup
4 eggs

1. Preheat oven to 350°F. Grease 1½-quart soufflé dish or round casserole.

2. Cook bacon in large skillet over medium-high heat about 7 minutes or until crisp. Drain bacon on paper towels; set aside. Reserve 2 tablespoons bacon drippings.

continued on page 16

Nutty Toffee Coffee Cake

Bacon and Maple Grits Puff, continued

3. Combine milk, water, grits and salt in medium saucepan. Bring to a boil over medium heat, stirring frequently. Reduce heat; simmer 2 to 3 minutes or until mixture thickens, stirring constantly. Remove from heat; stir in syrup and reserved 2 tablespoons bacon drippings.

4. Crumble bacon; reserve ¼ cup for garnish. Stir remaining crumbled bacon into grits mixture.

5. Beat eggs in medium bowl with electric mixer at high speed until thick and pale. Stir spoonful of grits mixture into eggs until well blended. Fold egg mixture into remaining grits mixture until blended; spoon into prepared casserole.

6. Bake 1 hour 20 minutes or until knife inserted into center comes out clean. Top with reserved ¼ cup bacon. Serve immediately.   *Makes 6 to 8 servings*

Note: Puff will fall slightly after being removed from the oven.

Delicious Ham & Cheese Puff Pie

    2 cups (about 1 pound) diced cooked ham
    1 package (10 ounces) frozen chopped spinach,
        thawed and squeezed dry
    ½ cup diced red bell pepper
    4 green onions, sliced
    3 eggs
    ¾ cup all-purpose flour
    ¾ cup (3 ounces) shredded Swiss cheese
    ¾ cup milk
    1 tablespoon prepared mustard
    1 teaspoon grated lemon peel
    1 teaspoon dried dill weed
    ½ teaspoon garlic salt
    ½ teaspoon black pepper
    Fresh dill sprigs and lemon slices (optional)

1. Preheat oven to 425°F. Grease round 2-quart casserole.

2. Combine ham, spinach, bell pepper and green onions in prepared casserole. Beat eggs in medium bowl. Stir in remaining ingredients except dill sprigs and lemon slices; pour over ham mixture.

3. Bake 30 to 35 minutes or until puffed and browned. Cut into wedges. Garnish with fresh dill and lemon slices.   *Makes 4 to 6 servings*

Delicious Ham & Cheese Puff Pie

Vegetarian Bounty

When you have eaten and are satisfied, praise the Lord . . . for the good land he has given you.

Deuteronomy 8:10 NIV

Veggie-Stuffed Portobello Mushrooms

- 4 large portobello mushrooms, about 1¼ to 1½ pounds
  Nonstick cooking spray
- 2 teaspoons olive oil or butter
- 1 cup chopped green or red bell pepper
- ⅓ cup sliced shallots or chopped onion
- 2 cloves garlic, minced
- 1 cup chopped zucchini or summer squash
- ½ teaspoon salt
- ¼ teaspoon black pepper
- 1 cup panko bread crumbs* or toasted fresh bread crumbs
- 1 cup shredded sharp Cheddar or mozzarella cheese

Panko bread crumbs are light, crispy, Japanese-style bread crumbs. They can be found in the Asian food aisle of most supermarkets.

1. Preheat broiler. Line baking sheet with foil. Gently remove mushroom stems; chop and set aside. Remove and discard brown gills from mushroom caps using spoon. Place mushroom caps top side up on prepared baking sheet. Coat lightly with cooking spray. Broil 4 to 5 inches from heat 5 minutes or until tender.

2. Meanwhile, heat oil in large nonstick skillet over medium-high heat. Add bell pepper, shallots and garlic; cook 5 minutes or until bell peppers begin to brown on edges, stirring occasionally. Stir in zucchini, reserved chopped mushroom stems, salt and black pepper; cook 3 to 4 minutes or until vegetables are tender, stirring frequently. Remove from heat; cool 5 minutes. Stir in bread crumbs and cheese.

3. Turn mushroom caps over. Mound vegetable mixture into caps. Return to broiler; broil 2 to 3 minutes or until golden brown and cheese is melted.

Makes 4 servings

Caramelized Onion Tart

- **2 tablespoons butter**
- **4 cups sliced onions**
- **½ teaspoon salt**
- **½ teaspoon dried thyme**
- **½ cup ORTEGA® Salsa**
- **2 tablespoons ORTEGA® Diced Jalapeños**
- **1 (9-inch) refrigerated unbaked pie crust**
- **½ cup shredded Cheddar cheese**

Preheat oven to 350°F. Melt butter in large saucepan over medium heat. Add onions, salt and thyme; stir to coat well. Cover; cook 5 minutes, stirring periodically to prevent onions from burning. Reduce heat; continue to cook and stir 15 minutes or until onions are golden brown and caramelized. Stir in salsa and jalapeños.

Place pie crust in 9-inch tart pan with removable bottom. Pierce dough several times with fork. Spread onion mixture evenly over crust.

Bake 20 minutes or until crust begins to brown on sides. Sprinkle cheese evenly over tart. Bake 5 minutes longer. Remove from oven; let stand 5 minutes. Carefully remove from tart pan. Serve warm or at room temperature. *Makes 6 to 8 servings*

Prep Time: 20 minutes
Start to Finish: 1 hour

For a great lunch or dinner item, use ORTEGA® Salsa Verde in the tart filling and serve it with a salad of mixed greens.

Quinoa-Stuffed Tomatoes

½ cup quinoa
3 cups water
½ teaspoon salt, divided
1 tablespoon olive oil
1 medium red bell pepper, chopped
⅓ cup chopped green onion
⅛ teaspoon black pepper
⅛ teaspoon dried thyme
1 tablespoon butter
8 plum tomatoes,* halved lengthwise, seeded, hollowed out

*Or substitute 4 medium tomatoes.

1. Preheat oven to 325°F. Place quinoa in fine-mesh sieve. Rinse well under cold running water. Bring 3 cups water and ¼ teaspoon salt to a boil in small saucepan. Stir in quinoa. Cover; reduce heat to low. Simmer 12 to 14 minutes or until quinoa is tender and plump. Drain well; set aside.

2. Heat oil in large skillet over medium-high heat. Add bell pepper; cook and stir 7 to 10 minutes or until tender. Stir in quinoa, green onion, remaining ¼ teaspoon salt, black pepper and thyme. Add butter; stir until melted. Remove from heat.

3. Arrange tomato halves in baking dish. Spoon in quinoa mixture. Bake 15 to 20 minutes or until tomatoes are tender. *Makes 8 servings*

Spicy Jac Mac & Cheese with Broccoli

2 cups (8 ounces) dry elbow macaroni
2 cups chopped fresh or frozen broccoli
2 cups (8 ounces) shredded sharp Cheddar cheese
2 cups (8 ounces) shredded Pepper Jack cheese*
1 can (12 fluid ounces) NESTLÉ® CARNATION® Evaporated Milk
½ cup grated Parmesan cheese, divided
½ teaspoon ground black pepper
2 tablespoons bread crumbs

*For a less spicy version, substitute 2 cups (8 ounces) shredded Monterey Jack cheese and a few dashes of hot pepper sauce (optional) for Pepper Jack cheese.

continued on page 24

Spicy Jac Mac & Cheese with Broccoli, continued

Preheat oven to 350°F. Lightly butter 2½-quart casserole dish.

Cook macaroni in large saucepan according to package directions, adding broccoli to boiling pasta water for last 3 minutes of cooking time; drain.

Combine cooked pasta, broccoli, Cheddar cheese, Pepper Jack cheese, evaporated milk, ¼ cup Parmesan cheese and black pepper in large bowl. Pour into prepared casserole dish. Combine remaining Parmesan cheese and bread crumbs; sprinkle over macaroni mixture. Cover tightly with aluminum foil.

Bake, covered, for 20 minutes. Remove foil; bake for additional 10 minutes or until lightly browned. *Makes 8 servings*

Wild Rice, Mushroom and Cranberry Dressing

>   3 cups water
>   1 teaspoon salt, divided
>   1 cup wild rice
>   1 tablespoon olive oil
>   1 cup chopped mushrooms*
>   1 small red onion, finely chopped
>   1 celery rib, finely chopped
>   ½ cup dried sweetened cranberries
>   ½ cup chopped toasted pecans (optional)**
>   ½ teaspoon minced fresh sage *or* ⅛ teaspoon dried sage
>   ⅛ teaspoon black pepper

*Shiitake mushrooms are preferred, but you may use your favorite mushroom variety.

**To toast pecans, spread in single layer in heavy-bottomed skillet. Cook over medium heat 1 to 2 minutes, stirring frequently, until nuts are lightly browned. Remove from skillet immediately. Cool before using.

1. Preheat oven to 325°F. Grease 2-quart casserole. Bring water and ½ teaspoon salt to a boil in medium saucepan. Stir in wild rice. Cover; reduce heat to low. Cook 45 minutes or until tender. Drain well.

2. Heat olive oil in large skillet over medium heat. Add mushrooms, onion and celery. Cook and stir 7 to 10 minutes or until tender. Stir in wild rice, cranberries, pecans, if desired, remaining ½ teaspoon salt, sage and pepper.

3. Spoon mixture into prepared casserole dish. Bake 20 minutes.

Makes 8 servings

Wild Rice, Mushroom and Cranberry Dressing

Veggie and Cheese Manicotti

1 jar (23 ounces) marinara sauce
1 package (8 ounces) manicotti
1 tablespoon olive or vegetable oil
1 cup fresh or frozen chopped broccoli
1 cup finely chopped mushrooms (optional)
½ cup shredded carrot
1 teaspoon minced garlic
1 container (15 ounces) ricotta cheese
1½ cups shredded mozzarella cheese, divided
2 eggs, lightly beaten
1 teaspoon Italian seasoning or oregano
1 teaspoon salt

1. Preheat oven to 350°F. Spray 13×9-inch baking dish with cooking spray. Spread about ¾ cup marinara sauce into baking dish; set aside. Cook manicotti according to package directions. Drain and rinse pasta in cool water; set aside.

2. Heat oil in large skillet over medium heat. Add broccoli, mushrooms, if desired, carrot, garlic and 2 tablespoons water. Cook about 8 minutes, stirring frequently, until vegetables are crisp-tender and water has evaporated.

3. Place vegetables in large bowl. Stir in ricotta, 1 cup mozzarella, eggs, Italian seasoning and salt. Fill each manicotti with vegetable-cheese mixture. Arrange filled manicotti in prepared baking dish. Pour remaining sauce over top and sprinkle with remaining ½ cup mozzarella.

4. Bake 55 minutes or until edges are browned and bubbly.   *Makes 6 to 7 servings*

Prep Time: 25 minutes
Bake Time: 55 minutes

Parmesan Vegetable Bake

½ cup seasoned dry bread crumbs
½ cup grated Parmesan cheese
2 tablespoons butter, cut into small pieces
1 clove garlic, minced
1 teaspoon dried oregano
¼ teaspoon black pepper
1 large baking potato, cut into ¼-inch-thick slices
1 medium zucchini, diagonally cut into ¼-inch-thick slices
1 large tomato, cut into ¼-inch-thick slices

1. Preheat oven to 375°F. Spray shallow 1-quart casserole with nonstick cooking spray.

2. Combine bread crumbs, cheese, butter, garlic, oregano and pepper in small bowl; mix well. Arrange potato slices in prepared casserole, overlapping slightly. Sprinkle with one third of crumb mixture. Top with zucchini slices; sprinkle with one third of crumb mixture. Top with tomato slices. Sprinkle with remaining crumb mixture.

3. Cover; bake 40 minutes. Remove cover; bake additional 10 minutes or until vegetables are tender. *Makes 4 servings*

Baked Bow-Tie Pasta in Mushroom Cream Sauce

- 1 teaspoon olive oil
- 1 large onion, thinly sliced
- 1 package (10 ounces) sliced mushrooms
- ⅛ teaspoon ground black pepper
- 1 jar (1 pound) RAGÚ® Cheesy!® Light Parmesan Alfredo Sauce
- 8 ounces bow tie pasta, cooked and drained
- 1 tablespoon grated Parmesan cheese
- 1 tablespoon plain dry bread crumbs (optional)

1. Preheat oven to 400°F. In 10-inch nonstick skillet, heat olive oil over medium heat and cook onion, mushrooms and pepper, stirring frequently, 10 minutes or until vegetables are golden. Stir in Ragú Cheesy! Sauce.

2. In 2-quart shallow baking dish, combine sauce mixture with hot pasta. Sprinkle with cheese combined with bread crumbs. Cover with aluminum foil and bake 20 minutes. Remove foil and bake an additional 5 minutes. *Makes 6 servings*

Prep Time: 10 minutes
Cook Time: 35 minutes

Black Bean Flautas with Charred Tomatillo Salsa

Salsa
- 1 pound tomatillos, unpeeled
- 1 small yellow onion, unpeeled
- 6 cloves garlic, unpeeled
- 1 jalapeño pepper*
  Juice of ½ lime
  Salt and black pepper

Flautas
- 1 can (15 ounces) black beans, undrained
- 1 cup vegetable broth
- 1 teaspoon salt, divided
- ½ teaspoon ground cumin
- ½ teaspoon chili powder
- 3 cloves garlic, peeled and minced
- ¼ cup chopped cilantro
  Juice of 1 lime
- 10 flour tortillas
- 2½ cups shredded Colby Jack cheese
- 1 cup seeded and chopped tomatoes (about 2 tomatoes)
- 1 cup thinly sliced green onions

*Jalapeño peppers can sting and irritate the skin, so wear rubber gloves when handling peppers and do not touch your eyes.

1. For salsa, cook and stir tomatillos, onion, garlic and jalapeño in large, heavy, dry skillet over medium-high heat about 20 minutes or until soft and skins are blackened. Remove from skillet; allow to cool 5 minutes. Peel tomatillos, onion and garlic, and remove stem and seeds from jalapeño. Place in blender or food processor with lime juice. Blend until smooth. Season to taste with salt and pepper. Set aside.

2. For flautas, place beans and liquid, broth, ½ teaspoon salt, cumin, chili powder and garlic in medium saucepan. Bring to a boil over medium-high heat. Reduce heat; simmer 10 minutes or until beans are very soft. Drain, reserving liquid. Purée drained bean mixture with cilantro, remaining ½ teaspoon salt and lime juice in blender or food processor until smooth. (Add reserved liquid 1 teaspoon at a time if beans are dry.)

3. Preheat oven to 450°F. Spread bean purée evenly on each tortilla; sprinkle with cheese, tomatoes and green onions. Roll up very tightly and place seam-side down in 13×9-inch baking dish. Bake 10 to 15 minutes or until crisp and brown and cheese is melted. Serve with salsa. *Makes 5 servings and 2 cups salsa*

Black Bean Flautas with Charred Tomatillo Salsa

Rio Bravo Rice-Stuffed Poblanos

6 large poblano peppers*
   Cooking oil
3 cups cooked long grain rice
²⁄₃ cup sour cream
1½ cups shredded smoked Gouda or Cheddar cheese, divided
1 cup frozen corn kernels, thawed
⅓ cup chopped cilantro leaves plus additional for garnish
   Salt and pepper to taste

*Poblano peppers can sting and irritate the skin, so wear rubber gloves when handling peppers and do not touch your eyes.

Preheat oven to 400°F. Slit each pepper lengthwise so peppers can later be stuffed with rice filling. Carefully remove loose seeds and veins, keeping stem intact. Rub pepper generously with oil and place on baking sheet. Combine rice, sour cream, 1 cup cheese, corn and cilantro in a medium bowl. Season with salt and pepper. Divide mixture to stuff each pepper; sprinkle with remaining cheese. Bake in preheated oven 20 to 25 minutes or until peppers are crisp-tender and filling is heated through. Garnish with cilantro.   *Makes 6 servings*

Favorite recipe from **USA Rice**

Divine Meats

*Go, eat your food with gladness, and drink . . .
with a joyful heart.*   Ecclesiastes 9:7 *NIV*

It's a Keeper Casserole

 1 tablespoon vegetable oil
½ cup chopped onion
¼ cup chopped green bell pepper
 1 clove garlic, minced
 2 tablespoons all-purpose flour
 1 teaspoon sugar
½ teaspoon salt
½ teaspoon dried basil
½ teaspoon black pepper
 1 package (about 16 ounces) frozen meatballs, cooked
 1 can (about 14 ounces) whole tomatoes, cut up and drained
1½ cups cooked vegetables (any combination)
 1 teaspoon beef bouillon granules
 1 teaspoon Worcestershire sauce
 1 can refrigerated buttermilk biscuits

1. Preheat oven to 400°F. Heat oil in large saucepan. Cook and stir onion, bell pepper and garlic over medium heat until vegetables are tender.

2. Stir in flour, sugar, salt, basil and black pepper. Slowly blend in meatballs, tomatoes, vegetables, bouillon and Worcestershire sauce. Cook and stir until slightly thickened and bubbly; pour into 2-quart casserole.

3. Unroll biscuits; place on top of casserole. Bake 15 minutes or until biscuits are golden.   *Makes 4 servings*

Old-Fashioned Turkey Pot Pie

**1 package (18 ounces) JENNIE-O TURKEY STORE® SO EASY Turkey
   Breast Chunks In Homestyle Gravy**
1½ cups frozen mixed vegetables, thawed
⅛ teaspoon black pepper
1 package (15 ounces) refrigerated pie crust, divided

Preheat oven to 350°F.

In large bowl, combine turkey breast chunks in gravy, vegetables and pepper.

Place one pie crust in bottom and up side of 9-inch pie plate. Spoon turkey and vegetable mixture over crust. Place top crust over filling. Fold edges of crust inward and flute as desired to seal.

Bake 50 to 55 minutes or until crust is golden brown.

Cut into wedges and serve. *Makes 4 servings*

Sausage Pizza Pie Casserole

8 ounces mild Italian sausage, casings removed
1 package (about 14 ounces) refrigerated pizza dough
½ cup tomato sauce
2 tablespoons chopped fresh basil *or* 2 teaspoons dried basil
½ teaspoon dried oregano
¼ teaspoon red pepper flakes
3 ounces whole mushrooms, quartered
½ cup thinly sliced red onion
½ cup thinly sliced green bell pepper
½ cup seeded diced tomato
½ cup sliced pitted black olives
8 slices smoked provolone cheese
2 tablespoons grated Parmesan and Romano cheese blend

1. Preheat oven to 350°F. Coat 13×9-inch baking dish with nonstick cooking spray.

2. Heat large skillet over medium-high heat. Add sausage; cook until browned, stirring frequently to break up meat. Drain fat.

3. Line prepared dish with pizza dough. Spoon sauce evenly over dough; sprinkle with basil, oregano and pepper flakes. Layer with sausage, mushrooms, onion, bell pepper, tomato, olives and provolone cheese. Roll down sides of crust to form rim. Bake 20 to 25 minutes or until bottom and sides of crust are golden brown. Sprinkle with cheese blend; let stand 5 minutes before serving. *Makes 4 to 6 servings*

Southwestern Enchiladas

1 can (10 ounces) enchilada sauce, divided
2 packages (about 6 ounces each) refrigerated fully-cooked steak strips*
4 (8-inch) flour tortillas
½ cup condensed nacho cheese soup, undiluted *or* ½ cup chile-flavored
pasteurized process cheese spread
1½ cups (6 ounces) shredded Mexican cheese blend

*Fully cooked steak strips can be found in the refrigerated prepared meats section of the supermarket.

1. Preheat oven to 350°F. Spread half of enchilada sauce in 9-inch square glass baking dish.

2. Place about half of one package steak down center of each tortilla. Top with 2 tablespoons cheese soup. Roll up tortillas; place seam side down in baking dish. Pour remaining enchilada sauce evenly over tortillas. Sprinkle with cheese. Bake 20 to 25 minutes or until heated through. *Makes 4 servings*

Mexican Tossed Layer Casserole

1 cup uncooked rice
12 ounces ground beef
¾ cup mild picante sauce
1 teaspoon ground cumin
2 cups shredded sharp Cheddar cheese, divided
½ cup sour cream
⅓ cup finely chopped green onion
2 tablespoons chopped cilantro
½ teaspoon salt
⅛ teaspoon ground red pepper

1. Preheat oven to 350°F. Coat 11×7-inch baking dish with nonstick cooking spray.

2. Cook rice according to package directions. Meanwhile, brown beef 6 to 8 minutes over medium-high heat, stirring to break up meat. Drain fat. Add picante sauce and cumin; stir well. Set aside.

3. Remove cooked rice from heat. Add 1 cup cheese, sour cream, green onion, cilantro, salt and red pepper. Toss gently and thoroughly to blend.

4. Spoon rice mixture into prepared baking dish. Top with beef mixture. Cover with foil. Bake 20 minutes or until heated through. Sprinkle with remaining 1 cup cheese. Bake uncovered 3 minutes more or until cheese is melted. *Makes 4 servings*

Heartland Chicken Casserole

10 slices white bread, cubed
1½ cups cracker crumbs or dry bread crumbs, divided
4 cups cubed cooked chicken
3 cups chicken broth
1 cup chopped onion
1 cup chopped celery
1 can (8 ounces) sliced mushrooms, drained
1 jar (about 4 ounces) pimientos, diced
3 eggs, lightly beaten
Salt and black pepper
1 tablespoon butter

1. Preheat oven to 350°F.

2. Combine bread cubes and 1 cup cracker crumbs in large bowl. Add chicken, broth, onion, celery, mushrooms, pimientos and eggs; mix well. Season with salt and pepper; spoon into 2½-quart casserole.

3. Melt butter in small saucepan. Add remaining ½ cup cracker crumbs; cook and stir until light brown. Sprinkle crumbs over casserole.

4. Bake 1 hour or until bubbly and heated through.   *Makes 6 servings*

Glass and ceramic bakeware absorb heat more slowly, making them great choices for casseroles and acidic foods.

Rainbow Casserole

5 potatoes, peeled and cut into thin slices
1 pound ground beef
1 onion, halved and thinly sliced
   Salt and black pepper
1 can (about 28 ounces) stewed tomatoes, drained, juice reserved
1 cup frozen peas

1. Preheat oven to 350°F. Spray 3-quart casserole with nonstick cooking spray.

2. Combine potatoes and enough salted water to cover in large saucepan. Bring to a boil. Boil, uncovered, 20 to 25 minutes or until potatoes are almost tender. Drain. Meanwhile, brown beef 6 to 8 minutes in large skillet over medium-high heat, stirring to break up meat. Drain fat.

3. Layer half of ground beef, half of potatoes, half of onion, salt, pepper, half of tomatoes and half of peas in prepared casserole. Repeat layers. Add reserved tomato juice.

4. Bake, covered, about 40 minutes or until most liquid is absorbed.

Makes 4 to 6 servings

Turkey and Mushroom Wild Rice Casserole

2 tablespoons butter
1 cup sliced fresh mushrooms *or* 1 can (4 ounces) sliced mushrooms
1 small onion, chopped
1 stalk celery, chopped
2 cups diced cooked turkey breast
1 can (about 10¾ ounces) condensed cream of mushroom soup,
    undiluted
1 pouch (about 9 ounces) ready-to-serve wild rice
1 cup milk
2 tablespoons minced fresh chives
¼ teaspoon black pepper
½ cup chopped pecans

1. Preheat oven to 350°F. Melt butter in large nonstick skillet over medium heat. Add mushrooms, onion and celery; cook 5 minutes or until onion is translucent. Stir in turkey, soup, rice, milk, chives and pepper; mix well.

2. Spoon mixture into 2-quart baking dish. Sprinkle with pecans. Bake 15 to 18 minutes or until bubbly and heated through.

Makes 4 servings

Spicy Chicken Casserole with Corn Bread

2 tablespoons olive oil
4 boneless skinless chicken breasts, cut into bite-size pieces
1 package (about 1 ounce) taco seasoning mix
1 can (about 15 ounces) black beans, rinsed and drained
1 can (about 14 ounces) diced tomatoes, drained
1 can (about 10 ounces) Mexican-style corn, drained
1 can (about 4 ounces) diced mild green chiles, drained
½ cup mild salsa
1 box (about 8 ounces) corn bread mix, plus ingredients to prepare mix
½ cup (2 ounces) shredded Cheddar cheese
¼ cup chopped red bell pepper

1. Preheat oven to 350°F. Spray 2-quart casserole with nonstick cooking spray. Heat oil in large skillet over medium heat. Cook chicken until no longer pink in center.

2. Sprinkle taco seasoning over chicken. Add black beans, tomatoes, corn, chiles and salsa; stir until well blended. Transfer to prepared dish.

3. Prepare corn bread mix according to package directions, adding cheese and bell pepper. Spread batter over chicken mixture.

4. Bake 30 minutes or until corn bread is golden brown. *Makes 4 to 6 servings*

Tortilla Beef Casserole

1 package (about 17 ounces) refrigerated fully cooked beef pot roast in gravy*
6 (6-inch) corn tortillas, cut into 1-inch pieces
1 jar (16 ounces) salsa
1½ cups corn
1 cup canned black or pinto beans, rinsed and drained
1 cup (4 ounces) shredded Mexican cheese blend

*Fully cooked beef pot roast can be found in the refrigerated prepared meats section of the supermarket.

1. Preheat oven to 350°F. Lightly spray 11×7-inch casserole or 2-quart casserole with nonstick cooking spray.

2. Drain and discard gravy from pot roast; cut or shred beef into bite-size pieces.

3. Combine beef, tortillas, salsa, corn and beans in large bowl; mix well. Transfer to prepared casserole. Bake 20 minutes or until heated through. Sprinkle with cheese; bake 5 minutes or until cheese is melted. *Makes 4 servings*

Spicy Chicken Casserole with Corn Bread

Layered Pasta Casserole

8 ounces uncooked penne pasta
8 ounces mild Italian sausage, casings removed
8 ounces ground beef
1 jar (about 26 ounces) pasta sauce
2 cups (8 ounces) shredded mozzarella cheese, divided
1 package (10 ounces) frozen chopped spinach, thawed and squeezed dry
1 cup whole milk ricotta cheese
½ cup grated Parmesan cheese
1 egg
2 tablespoons chopped fresh basil *or* 2 teaspoons dried basil
1 teaspoon salt

1. Preheat oven to 350°F. Spray 13×9-inch baking dish with nonstick cooking spray. Cook pasta according to package directions; drain. Transfer to prepared dish.

2. Meanwhile, cook sausage and ground beef in large skillet over medium-high heat until browned, stirring to break up meat. Drain fat. Add pasta sauce; mix well. Add half of meat sauce to pasta; toss to coat.

3. Combine 1 cup mozzarella, spinach, ricotta, Parmesan, egg, basil and salt in medium bowl. Spoon small mounds of spinach mixture over pasta mixture; spread evenly with back of spoon. Top with remaining meat sauce; sprinkle with remaining 1 cup mozzarella. Bake 30 minutes.   *Makes 6 to 8 servings*

Creamy Chile and Chicken Casserole

3 tablespoons butter, divided
2 jalapeño peppers,* seeded and finely chopped
2 tablespoons all-purpose flour
½ cup whipping cream
1 cup chicken broth
1 cup (4 ounces) shredded sharp Cheddar cheese
1 cup (4 ounces) shredded Asiago cheese
1 cup sliced mushrooms
1 yellow squash, chopped
1 red bell pepper, chopped
1 stalk celery, chopped
12 ounces diced cooked chicken breast
¼ cup chopped green onions
¼ teaspoon salt
¼ teaspoon black pepper
½ cup sliced almonds

Jalapeño peppers can sting and irritate the skin, so wear rubber gloves when handling peppers and do not touch your eyes.

1. Preheat oven to 350°F. Melt 2 tablespoons butter in medium saucepan. Add jalapeños; cook and stir 1 minute over high heat. Add flour; stir to make paste. Add cream; stir until thickened. Add broth; stir until smooth. Gradually add cheeses; stir until melted.

2. Melt remaining 1 tablespoon butter in large skillet. Add mushrooms, squash, bell pepper and celery. Cook and stir over high heat 3 to 5 minutes or until vegetables are tender. Remove from heat. Stir in chicken, green onions, salt and black pepper. Stir in cheese sauce.

3. Spoon mixture into shallow 2-quart casserole dish. Sprinkle with almonds. Bake 10 minutes or until casserole is bubbly and heated through.   *Makes 6 servings*

Pork and Corn Bread Stuffing Casserole

½ teaspoon paprika
¼ teaspoon salt
¼ teaspoon garlic powder
¼ teaspoon black pepper
4 bone-in pork chops (about 1¾ pounds)
2 tablespoons butter
1½ cups chopped onions
¾ cup thinly sliced celery
¾ cup matchstick carrots*
¼ cup chopped fresh parsley
1 can (about 14 ounces) chicken broth
4 cups corn bread stuffing

*Matchstick carrots are sometimes called shredded carrots and are sold with other prepared vegetables in the supermarket produce section.

1. Preheat oven to 350°F. Lightly coat 13×9-inch baking dish with nonstick cooking spray.

2. Combine paprika, salt, garlic powder and pepper in small bowl. Season both sides of pork chops with paprika mixture.

3. Melt butter in large skillet over medium-high heat. Add pork chops; cook 2 minutes or just until browned. Turn; cook 1 minute. Transfer to plate; set aside.

4. Add onions, celery, carrots and parsley to skillet. Cook and stir 4 minutes or until onions are translucent. Add broth; bring to a boil over high heat. Remove from heat; add stuffing and fluff with fork.

5. Transfer mixture to prepared baking dish. Place pork chops on top. Cover; bake 25 minutes or until pork is no longer pink in center.   *Makes 4 servings*

Super Salads

They broke bread in their homes and ate together with glad and sincere hearts. Acts 2:46 NIV

Very Verde Green Bean Salad

- 1 tablespoon olive oil
- 1 pound fresh green beans
- ½ cup water
- ½ teaspoon salt
- ½ teaspoon black pepper
- ½ cup ORTEGA® Salsa Verde
- 2 tablespoons ORTEGA® Garden Vegetable Salsa

Heat oil in large skillet over medium heat. When oil begins to shimmer, add green beans; toss lightly in oil. Heat about 3 minutes, tossing to coat beans well.

Add water, salt and pepper carefully. Cover; cook 5 minutes or until beans are tender. Add salsas; toss to coat beans evenly. Heat 1 or 2 minutes to warm salsas. Refrigerate or serve at room temperature. *Makes 4 servings*

Prep Time: 5 minutes
Start to Finish: 15 minutes

Cran-Raspberry Gelatin Salad

2 cups boiling water
1 package (4-serving size) cranberry gelatin
1 package (4-serving size) raspberry gelatin
1 can (16 ounces) jellied cranberry sauce
1 tablespoon lemon juice
4 cups frozen raspberries, thawed and drained
1 cup chopped walnuts

1. Coat 1 (2-quart) ring mold with nonstick cooking spray; place on baking sheet.

2. Combine boiling water and gelatins in large bowl; stir until dissolved. Melt cranberry sauce in medium saucepan over low heat about 5 minutes. Add cranberry sauce and lemon juice to gelatin mixture; whisk until smooth. Fold in raspberries and walnuts. Pour into prepared mold. Cover and refrigerate about 6 hours or until firm.

Makes 12 servings

Potato, Cucumber and Dill Salad

3 large IDAHO® Potatoes, unpeeled and thinly sliced
¼ cup rice wine vinegar
1½ tablespoons Dijon mustard
¼ cup canola or vegetable oil
½ cup chopped fresh dill, *or* 1 tablespoon dried whole dill weed
½ teaspoon salt
1 large cucumber, unpeeled and thinly sliced

1. Place potato slices in a 9-inch square microwave-safe baking dish; cover with microwaveable plastic wrap and microwave on HIGH 9 to 11 minutes or until tender, stirring gently every 3 minutes.

2. Combine vinegar, mustard, oil, dill and salt in a small jar. Cover tightly and shake vigorously. Pour vinegar mixture over potatoes. Cover and refrigerate until chilled. Gently mix in sliced cucumber before serving.

Makes 4 servings

A baked potato is done when it reaches an internal temperature of 210°F.

Nine-Layer Salad

6 cups packed baby spinach
1½ cups grape tomatoes
2 cups pattypan squash, halved crosswise
1 cup peas, blanched
4 ounces baby corn, halved lengthwise
2 cups baby carrots, blanched and halved lengthwise
1 cup peppercorn ranch salad dressing
1 cup shredded Cheddar cheese
4 strips bacon

1. Layer spinach, tomatoes, squash, peas, corn and carrots in 4-quart glass bowl. Pour dressing over salad; spread evenly. Top with cheese. Cover and refrigerate 4 hours.

2. Cook bacon in medium skillet over medium-high heat until crispy. Crumble and sprinkle over top of salad. *Makes 7 servings*

Southwest Pasta Salad

12 ounces tricolor rotini
1 can (15 ounces) kidney beans, drained and rinsed
1 can (11 ounces) whole kernel corn, drained
⅓ cup chopped red pepper
⅓ cup chopped green pepper
3 green onions, chopped
1 cup oil-free Italian salad dressing
2 to 3 tablespoons salad seasoning
¾ cup grated Cheddar cheese

Prepare pasta according to package directions; rinse with cold water and drain. In large bowl combine pasta, beans, corn, red and green pepper and onion. Mix salad dressing with salad seasoning and add to pasta mixture. Add cheese and toss. Refrigerate 3 to 4 hours to blend flavors. Add additional salad dressing if desired. *Makes 6 servings*

Favorite recipe from **North Dakota Wheat Commission**

Sesame Rice Salad

1 can (15 ounces) mandarin orange segments, undrained
1 teaspoon ground ginger
2 cups MINUTE® Brown Rice, uncooked
½ cup Asian sesame salad dressing
3 green onions, thinly sliced
1 can (8 ounces) sliced water chestnuts, drained and chopped
½ cup sliced celery

Drain oranges, reserving liquid. Add enough water to reserved liquid to measure 1¾ cups. Stir in ginger. Prepare rice according to package directions, substituting 1¾ cups orange liquid for water. Refrigerate cooked rice 30 minutes. Add dressing, onions, water chestnuts and celery; mix lightly. Gently stir in oranges.

Makes 4 servings

Loaded, Baked Potato Salad

4 pounds IDAHO® potatoes, peeled
1 pound bacon, crisply cooked, and chopped into
    ½-inch pieces (fat reserved, if desired)
4 ounces unsalted butter, softened
½ cup chopped green onions
2 cups grated or shredded Cheddar cheese
1½ cups sour cream (regular or low-fat)
1 tablespoon black pepper
1 teaspoon salt

1. Cook whole potatoes in boiling, unsalted water until tender. Refrigerate until chilled, then chop into 1-inch pieces.

2. Transfer the potatoes to a large bowl along with the remaining ingredients and thoroughly combine. Add some of the reserved bacon fat if desired.

3. Chill at least 2 hours before serving. Adjust the seasoning prior to serving.

Makes 2 quarts

Note: Any condiments or toppings typically added to a loaded baked potato may be used for this recipe.

Roasted Sweet Potato Salad

2 pounds sweet potatoes or yams, peeled and cut into ½-inch cubes
¾ cup HELLMANN'S® or BEST FOODS® Canola Cholesterol Free
**   Mayonnaise, divided**
1 medium Granny Smith apple, cored and cut into ¼-inch cubes
½ cup dried cranberries

1. Preheat oven to 400°F.

2. In medium bowl, toss potatoes with 2 tablespoons HELLMANN'S® or BEST FOODS® Canola Cholesterol Free Mayonnaise. On baking sheet, evenly spread potatoes.

3. Bake, stirring once, 30 minutes or until potatoes are tender; cool completely.

4. In large bowl, combine potatoes, apple, cranberries and remaining Mayonnaise; toss to coat. Chill, if desired.   *Makes 10 servings*

Prep Time: 20 minutes
Chill Time: 30 minutes

For an extra special twist, add sweetened pecans. In 12-inch nonstick skillet, cook 1 cup chopped pecans with 6 tablespoons sugar, stirring constantly, 5 minutes or until sugar browns. Spread pecan mixture onto greased aluminum foil. Let cool. Break into bite-size pieces and add to salad just before serving.

Fiesta Pasta Salad

12 ounces tricolor rotini pasta
1 cup ORTEGA® Garden Vegetable Salsa
¼ cup mayonnaise
1 cup frozen whole-kernel corn, thawed
1 cup JOAN OF ARC® Black Beans, drained
2 tablespoons ORTEGA® Diced Jalapeños
3 green onions, diced
½ cup chopped fresh cilantro

Cook pasta according to package directions. Cool.

Combine pasta, salsa, mayonnaise, corn, beans, jalapeños, green onions and cilantro in large bowl; mix well. Refrigerate at least 30 minutes before serving.

Makes 6 to 8 servings

Prep Time: 5 minutes
Start to Finish: 45 minutes

Pesto Rice Salad

2 cups MINUTE® White Rice, uncooked
1 package (7 ounces) basil pesto sauce
1 cup cherry tomatoes, halved
8 ounces whole-milk mozzarella cheese, cut into ½-inch cubes
⅓ cup shredded Parmesan cheese
Toasted pine nuts (optional)

Prepare rice according to package directions. Place in large bowl. Let stand
10 minutes. Add pesto sauce; mix well. Gently stir in tomatoes and cheese. Serve
warm or cover and refrigerate until ready to serve. Sprinkle with pine nuts, if desired.

Makes 6 servings

To toast pine nuts, spread in single layer in heavy-bottomed skillet. Cook over medium heat 1 to 2 minutes, stirring frequently, until nuts are lightly browned. Remove from skillet immediately. Cool before using.

Pounceole Salad

1 can (20 ounces) hominy
2 teaspoons water
1 can (15 ounces) JOAN OF ARC® Kidney Beans or pinto beans,
    drained, rinsed
1 can (15 ounces) yellow corn, drained
½ cup diced red bell pepper
½ cup diced red onion
3 tablespoons ORTEGA® Diced Green Chiles
½ teaspoon salt
½ teaspoon black pepper
½ cup ORTEGA® Original Salsa, Medium

Pour hominy into skillet; add water. Cook over low heat; separate hominy with wooden spoon. Drain well. Place into large bowl. Add beans, corn, bell pepper, onion, chiles, salt and black pepper. Toss to combine well. Stir in salsa. Serve at room temperature or refrigerate up to 24 hours. *Makes 6 to 8 servings*

Variation: For additional color and an intriguing flavor, substitute cooked and shelled edamame for the beans.

Prep Time: 5 minutes
Start to Finish: 20 minutes

Tapioca Fruit Salad

1½ cups coconut milk
1 cup milk
¾ cup sugar, divided
2 eggs, beaten
¼ cup water
3 tablespoons quick-cooking tapioca
½ teaspoon vanilla
Pinch salt
2 cups fresh pineapple chunks
2 cups quartered fresh strawberries
1 cup diced mango
1 cup fresh blueberries
1 cup fresh blackberries
Grated peel of 1 lime
2 tablespoons lime juice

1. Mix coconut milk, milk, ½ cup sugar, eggs, water, tapioca, vanilla and salt in medium saucepan. Let stand 5 minutes. Bring to a boil over medium heat, stirring constantly. Remove from heat. Cool 30 minutes. (Pudding thickens as it cools.)

2. Spoon into individual dessert bowls. Combine pineapple, strawberries, mango, blueberries and blackberries in large bowl. Stir in remaining ¼ cup sugar, lime peel and juice; mix well. Spoon over tapioca.

3. Cover; refrigerate 2 to 3 hours before serving. *Makes 8 servings*

Seafood Feasts

The Family Table
Be known to us in breaking bread, but do not
then depart; Saviour, abide with us, and spread
Thy table in our heart. James Montgomery

Tuna Tomato Casserole

2 cans (6 ounces each) tuna, drained
1 cup mayonnaise
1 small onion, finely chopped
¼ teaspoon salt
¼ teaspoon black pepper
1 package (12 ounces) uncooked wide egg noodles
8 to 10 plum tomatoes, sliced ¼ inch thick
1 cup (4 ounces) shredded Cheddar or mozzarella cheese

1. Preheat oven to 375°F.

2. Combine tuna, mayonnaise, onion, salt and pepper in medium bowl; mix well.

3. Cook noodles according to package directions. Drain and return to saucepan. Stir tuna mixture into noodles until well blended.

4. Layer half of noodle mixture, half of tomatoes and half of cheese in 13×9-inch baking dish. Press down slightly. Repeat layers.

5. Bake 20 minutes or until cheese is melted and casserole is heated through.

Makes 6 servings

Lemon Shrimp

1 package (12 ounces) uncooked egg noodles
½ cup (1 stick) butter, softened
2 pounds medium cooked shrimp
3 tomatoes, chopped
1 cup *each* shredded carrots and chicken broth
1 can (4 ounces) sliced mushrooms, drained
2 tablespoons lemon juice
2 cloves garlic, chopped
½ teaspoon celery seed
¼ teaspoon black pepper

Preheat oven to 350°F. Cook noodles according to package directions. Drain; toss with butter in large bowl until butter is melted and noodles are evenly coated. Stir in remaining ingredients. Transfer to 3-quart casserole. Bake 15 to 20 minutes or until heated through. *Makes 8 servings*

Baked Red Snappers with Veg•All®

2 pounds red snapper
1 small onion, minced
½ green pepper, minced
1 jalapeño (with seeds), minced*
½ cup black olives, sliced
4 garlic cloves, minced
1 can (15 ounces) VEG•ALL® Original Mixed Vegetables, drained
2 cups cooked rice
½ teaspoon salt
¼ teaspoon pepper

Jalapeño peppers can sting and irritate the skin, so wear rubber gloves when handling peppers and do not touch your eyes.

Preheat oven to 400°F.

Lightly grease oven-proof casserole dish. Place snapper in casserole dish without crowding.

In medium bowl, mix onion, green pepper, jalapeño, black olives and garlic. Stir in Veg•All, rice, salt and pepper.

Lightly stuff cavities of snapper with filling. Place any remaining filling around snapper. Bake 20 minutes. *Makes 4 servings*

Crab-Artichoke Casserole

8 ounces uncooked small shell pasta
2 tablespoons butter
6 green onions, chopped
2 tablespoons all-purpose flour
1 cup half-and-half
1 teaspoon dry mustard
½ teaspoon ground red pepper
  Salt and black pepper
½ cup (2 ounces) shredded Swiss cheese, divided
1 package (about 8 ounces) imitation crabmeat
1 can (about 14 ounces) artichoke hearts, drained and cut
    into bite-size pieces

1. Preheat oven to 350°F. Grease 2-quart casserole. Cook pasta according to package directions; drain and set aside.

2. Melt butter in large saucepan over medium heat. Add green onions; cook and stir about 2 minutes. Add flour; cook and stir 2 minutes. Gradually add half-and-half, whisking constantly until mixture begins to thicken. Whisk in mustard and red pepper; season to taste with salt and black pepper. Remove from heat; stir in ¼ cup cheese until melted.

3. Combine crabmeat, artichokes and pasta in prepared casserole. Add sauce mixture; stir until blended. Top with remaining ¼ cup cheese. Bake about 40 minutes or until bubbly, lightly browned and heated through.   *Makes 6 servings*

Creamy Alfredo Seafood Lasagna

1 jar (1 pound) RAGÚ® Cheesy!® Classic Alfredo Sauce, divided
1 pound imitation crabmeat, separated into bite-sized pieces
1 container (15 ounces) ricotta cheese
2 cups shredded mozzarella cheese (about 8 ounces), divided
1 small onion, chopped
12 lasagna noodles, cooked and drained
2 tablespoons grated Parmesan cheese

1. Preheat oven to 350°F. In medium bowl, combine ½ cup Ragú Cheesy! Classic Alfredo Sauce, crabmeat, ricotta cheese, 1½ cups mozzarella cheese and onion; set aside.

continued on page 72

Crab-Artichoke Casserole

Creamy Alfredo Seafood Lasagna, continued

2. In 13×9-inch baking dish, spread ½ cup Pasta Sauce. Arrange 4 lasagna noodles, then top with ½ of ricotta mixture; repeat layers, ending with noodles. Top with remaining ½ cup sauce.

3. Cover with aluminum foil and bake 40 minutes. Remove foil and sprinkle with remaining ½ cup mozzarella cheese and Parmesan cheese. Bake an additional 10 minutes or until cheeses are melted. Let stand 10 minutes before serving.

Makes 8 servings

Prep Time: 25 minutes
Cook Time: 50 minutes

Crustless Salmon & Broccoli Quiche

- ¼ **cup chopped green onions**
- 3 **eggs**
- ¼ **cup plain yogurt**
- 2 **teaspoons all-purpose flour**
- 1 **teaspoon dried basil**
- ⅛ **teaspoon salt**
- ⅛ **teaspoon black pepper**
- ¾ **cup frozen broccoli florets, thawed and drained**
- ⅓ **cup (3 ounces) drained and flaked water-packed boneless skinless canned salmon**
- 2 **tablespoons grated Parmesan cheese**
- 1 **plum tomato, thinly sliced**
- ¼ **cup fresh bread crumbs**

1. Preheat oven to 375°F. Spray 1½-quart casserole or 9-inch deep-dish pie plate with nonstick cooking spray.

2. Combine green onions, eggs, yogurt, flour, basil, salt and pepper in medium bowl until well blended. Stir in broccoli, salmon and cheese. Spread evenly in prepared casserole. Top with tomato slices and sprinkle with bread crumbs.

3. Bake 20 to 25 minutes or until knife inserted into center comes out clean. Let stand 5 minutes. Cut in half before serving.

Makes 4 servings

Shrimp Primavera Pot Pie

1 can (10¾ ounces) condensed cream of shrimp soup, undiluted
1 package (12 ounces) frozen medium raw shrimp, peeled
2 packages (1 pound each) frozen mixed vegetables, such as green beans, potatoes, onions and red bell peppers, thawed and drained
1 teaspoon dried dill weed
¼ teaspoon salt
¼ teaspoon black pepper
1 package (11 ounces) refrigerated breadstick dough

1. Preheat oven to 400°F.

2. Heat soup in medium ovenproof skillet over medium-high heat 1 minute. Add shrimp; cook and stir 3 minutes or until shrimp begin to thaw. Stir in vegetables, dill, salt and pepper; mix well. Reduce heat to medium-low; cook and stir 3 minutes.

3. Unwrap breadstick dough; separate into 8 strips. Twist strips and arrange attractively over shrimp mixture in crisscross pattern, cutting to fit skillet. Press ends of dough lightly to edge of skillet to secure.

4. Bake 18 minutes or until crust is golden brown and shrimp mixture is bubbly and heated through. *Makes 4 to 6 servings*

Prep and Cook Time: 30 minutes

Paella

¼ cup **FILIPPO BERIO® Olive Oil**
1 pound **boneless skinless chicken breasts, cut into 1-inch strips**
½ pound **Italian sausage links, cut into 1-inch slices**
1 **onion, chopped**
3 cloves **garlic, minced**
2 (14½-ounce) cans **chicken broth**
2 cups **uncooked long grain white rice**
1 (8-ounce) bottle **clam juice**
1 (2-ounce) jar **chopped pimientos, drained**
2 **bay leaves**
1 teaspoon **salt**
¼ teaspoon **saffron threads, crumbled (optional)**
1 pound **raw shrimp, shelled and deveined**
1 (16-ounce) can **whole tomatoes, drained**
1 (10-ounce) package **frozen peas, thawed**
12 **littleneck clams, scrubbed**
¼ cup **water**
    Fresh herb sprig (optional)

Preheat oven to 350°F. In large skillet, heat olive oil over medium heat until hot. Add chicken; cook and stir 8 to 10 minutes or until brown on all sides. Remove with slotted spoon; set aside. Add sausage to skillet; cook and stir 8 to 10 minutes or until brown. Remove with slotted spoon; set aside. Add onion and garlic to skillet; cook and stir 5 to 7 minutes or until onion is tender. Transfer chicken, sausage, onion and garlic to large casserole.

Add chicken broth, rice, clam juice, pimientos, bay leaves, salt and saffron, if desired, to chicken mixture. Cover; bake 30 minutes. Add shrimp, tomatoes and peas; stir well. Cover; bake an additional 15 minutes or until rice is tender, liquid is absorbed and shrimp are opaque. Remove bay leaves.

Meanwhile, combine clams and water in stockpot or large saucepan. Cover; cook over medium heat 5 to 10 minutes or until clams open; remove clams immediately as they open. Discard any clams with unopened shells. Place clams on top of paella. Garnish with herb sprig, if desired.   *Makes 4 to 6 servings*

The publisher would like to thank the companies and organizations listed below for the use of their recipes and photographs in this publication.

Cream of Wheat® Cereal

Dole Food Company, Inc.

Filippo Berio® Olive Oil

The Hershey Company

Hillshire Farm®

Idaho Potato Commission

Jennie-O Turkey Store, LLC

Nestlé USA

North Dakota Wheat Commission

Ortega®, A Division of B&G Foods, Inc.

Riviana Foods Inc.

Unilever

USA Rice Federation®

Veg•All®